CW00517190

LANDSCAPE OF THE BODY

First published in 2023 by
The Dedalus Press
13 Moyclare Road
Baldoyle
Dublin D13 K1C2
Ireland

www.dedaluspress.com

ISBN 978-1-915629-19-7 (paperback)
ISBN 978-1-915629-18-0 (hardback)

Dedalus Press titles are available in Ireland
from Argosy Books (www.argosybooks.ie) and in the UK
from Inpress Books (www.inpressbooks.co.uk)
Printed in Dublin by Print Dynamics.

Cover image: *Untitled. _ Scape(s) #3.* mixed-media-on-paper,
145 x 120 cm, by Jennifer Smith (2013),
by kind permission of the artist.
www.jennifersmith.nl

The Dedalus Press receives financial assistance from
The Arts Council / An Chomhairle Ealaíon.

LANDSCAPE OF THE BODY

LANI O'HANLON

DEDALUS PRESS

CONTENTS

routes and rhythms

to keep walking is to swim against myself

⌒

body to body, breath in breath

⌒

drips of light, small claps of colour

ecstasy zinging through flesh, our blood

for my family
and Grace Wells

⁓

Between the head and feet of any given person
is a billion miles of unexplored wilderness.
— Gabrielle Roth

routes and rhythms

We Learn on Small Feet

*'We vibrate to the rhythms of our mother's blood … and this pulse
is the thread of blood that runs all the way back through the
grandmothers to the first mother.'*
— Layne Redmond, *When The Drummers Were Women:
A Spiritual History of Rhythm*

You often wore black and dieted on Mondays,
tap danced to pay the milk bill, the bread bill,

large bars of fruit and nut chocolate,
red lemonade on Sundays

watching Gene and Cyd, Fred and Ginger,
Sammy Davis Junior.

You stepped out across the stages of my childhood
in fish-net tights, top hat and cane.

In the Mood, Gotta Dance, Mr. Bojangles.

You worked your body hard

but you could catch any sequence, rhythm or sean-nós batter,
repeat it with the accuracy of genius

and we learnt on small feet how to punctuate
your rhythm with our own.

That rhythm, that rhythm,

the rocking sway and touch – of you – the pulse and breath
    and beat.

Cloud Readers

Daddy jigged and deedleee
deetle didle dummed into the front room
to make me laugh in my pram.

At age two, Mam posed me on a table,
dressed up in tulle and ballet shoes,
for a photographer from the *Echo*.

They called each other Hon.
Divined pictures from clouds in Glanmire,
'You see the owl there? The bull, you see?'

And before my sisters came along
we had glass animals on a coffee table;
a red deer, a blue monkey, a green horse.

Dad told me stories
about when he was a little boy
catching pigeons and fish with his hands.

Half-asleep in the auditorium
I'd watch them onstage
all sequinned up. Far away.

Cloud readers. Stars.

Making Huts

Given time I'd make a hut here
on this patch of ground beside the bridge.
Like the hut we made, Mags
and I on the green in Hazel Ave.

Two Foxford blankets around the trees;
tins, three; one for library money,
one for biscuits and one for stones.

We made a stage from an old pallet,
taught the other children how to read,
dance and sing. But we were the stars
when the parents came to our theatre.

We used that money to buy Lucky Bags,
a jam and cream sandwich. One of the boys,
Garry Welsh it was, I think, pushed
another boy and he fell onto the cake
but we ate it anyway – squashed as it was,
cream on mouths and fingers, cream and jam.

All summer we stayed away from our homes;
Mrs. Lynch pulling Mags's dark hair,
Dad waking us in the night to slap and shout,
we climbed through the bones of trees
and built a house from wool and leaves.

Autoroute

Dad and Mr Rush spread a map across the bonnet of the Cortina,
draw their fingers along the red and green snakes,
plotting a route through England to France and Spain;
Le Havre, Lyon, Paris, Poitiers, San Sebastian.

Mr. Rush is taller but Dad is better looking,
dark hair, brown eyes and strong teeth.
People think he is Italian or Spanish,
he is really pleased if they think he is Spanish.

We practise camping in Brittas Bay, all weekend the sky drizzles.
We drive into Gorey to see Teddy and Fossett's circus.
Dad tells us stories about travelling with the Fit-up Shows, himself
and Johnny Petrassi slapping each other with cakes made of
    shaving cream.

We set off into the sun, Dad's got the phrasebooks
in the glove compartment with the big map.
The boot packed with Andrews Liver Salts, tinned Spam
and beans in case we can't eat the food.

On the ferry we explore corridors, cubbyholes, cabins,
go out on deck, Emer's hair frizzing up in a gold brown halo.
Elaine and I in green sundresses, our hair is long. The deck is slippy.
He takes our photograph, the continent getting closer.

French bread, peaches, the blue sea.
Every year I am the navigator calling out turns on the map.
At age fifteen, I kiss a boy who works on the Waltzers. Back in the car
Dad shouts 'What were you thinking? Traipsing off with
    a fairground Johnny?'

In the mountains near Granada a gypsy
takes my hand, reads my future,
tracing lines and routes away from
and back again to family.

Woman with Grapes

The blue sea turns darker. Another vendor
comes through a tunnel in the cliff to the smaller beach –
round Madonna face, black dress, a basket of purple grapes.

The Spanish call out to her to buy a bunch.
The woman sees me watching, walks towards me,
between the tips of her fingers a twig

weighed down with grapes. She offers the fruit.
Dad shouts over at her *'Non, no pesetas.* No.'
She slaps the air back at him,

spits words 'No charge for her.'
then she leans towards me, eyes indigo
as the grapes drop fat and cool into my hand.

She sees my new breasts like secrets under my top –
the tight skin, the ache low down in my belly,
a burst of juice as I bite through to the flesh.

Duende

'… *duende is not in the throat: duende surges up, inside,
from the soles of the feet.*'
—Federico García Lorca, translation by A.S. Kline

An embarrassing lunch with the bus drivers
and one of the tour guides, your date, all of them speaking Spanish.

You twirl spaghetti around your fork.
One guy leans in close: 'You know he's married?'

The thick scent of aftershave is sickening
but there is another cathedral to see in Granada, then a gallery.

Just when you think it is over and you can flee
back to your mother, the bus begins to climb.

You step out into a mountain village drenched in light.
Wild-haired men zip past on scooters, fags hanging from their lips.

In a whitewashed cave house, those same men
play guitars, singing and flamenco clapping.

Women and girls stomp across the floor in battered shoes,
clicking fingers, and lifting skirts showing earth-stained legs.

On the walls, copper bowls and pans shine.
The women's eyes turn inward, rhythm scorching up through them.

A man draws his fingers across a guitar, a woman cries out
from belly and throat, a break in her voice; her intimate song.

The music stops and an older woman rises, lifts her chin,
    then her arms.
Single taps, double then treble, skipping in and out
    of the clapping, the castanets,

the clacking of her heels, hailstones on a tin roof, fast, so fast
only your blood can keep up. A man licks your breasts with his eyes.

You're fifteen and when you board the bus you're crying
as if everyone you ever loved, everything you ever loved, is dying.

Back Up Quick, They're Hippies

That was the year we drove
into a commune in Cornwall.
'Jesus, Jim,' Mam said,
'back-up quick, they're hippies.'

Through the car window,
tents, row after row, flaps open,
long-haired men and women
curled around each other like babies

and the babies themselves
toddled naked across the grass.

I reached for the handle, ready, almost,
to open the door, drop out and away
from my sister's kicking legs,
Dad ranting at other drivers.

Back home in the Dandelion market a busker taught me
how to play the Jew's harp with teeth, breath and tongue.
I tried to unlearn the Hollywood songs
and dances my mother taught.

Bought a headband, an afghan coat.
Barefoot, on common grass, I lay down with kin.

Sister

Your dark hair, newly washed,
thrown forward in front of the Superser,
earthy scent of henna in the heated air.

That swagger as you ingested straight vodka
or demonstrated the facts of life
with a Chef Sauce bottle.

The night you kicked Nellie Byrne
through the canvas tent in Kilmuckridge,
cause she stole your fella; Billy Casey.

As we galloped on pillows, then ponies
across fields and through woods,
you were always softer, braver.

Two itchy Aran hats,
two pairs of tap and ballet shoes,
two bikes whirring over concrete.

Your body next to mine in the double bed,
the line we drew down the middle;
your side | my side.

Can Speak

The pair of us in Tindle's wood looking for fairies
and treasure he conjured from twigs, leaves,
saucers of light.

The dirty greens of winter days
powdered with roses, reindeer moss,
finger salt and gold leaf. Breath rendered pink.

In spring, the rafters and corners of barns lifted so high
I could look down on bird's eggs, blue and green, fragile
as baby's nails.

Birdies, he said, can speak
if you slice their tongues
with a sixpence.

I didn't know then that Tindle's Wood
was a place where men hanged themselves.

I am trapped in that wood. A man approaching.

A Red Negligee in a White Vanity Case

After you found it, after that murder of a row in the night,

we woke to a morning without her.
My bedroom door creaked open like Dracula's coffin.
It was you, Dad, coming in to crouch and cry beside my bed.

One part of me wanted to comfort you,
smooth your wrinkled shirt and too long hair.
Another part of me wanted to shove, scream, thump.

'It's all your fault.'
But I patted your shelled back,
stared through dusty Venetian blinds, wishing

I could fly like the crows above our house
with all that it held.
And it held – she came back.

The Dutchman who loved her –
and he really loved her –
was sent away.

Mam sat alone at night with Smirnoff
and photographs of herself
on his yacht in Majorca,

our new Christmas dressing gowns, soft as fur.

A Note on the Edge

Driving to the hospital
I don't play music

though Leonard Cohen's last CD
is in the pocket of the car door

with it all getting darker
and the treaty needed

between your love and mine.
I don't play music

though Ludovico Einaudi is waiting,
hands poised above the piano keys,

the way yours used to be
before you played the Nocturnes—

Chopin, John Field.
I don't play

but the frosted trees strike
the rim of the sky like a bell

or a note on the edge
of a Tibetan singing bowl.

And another part of me
is kneeling down to pray.

Autoroute 2

You buy a campervan, Dad, the week before you die.
By the time I get to the hospital you're unconscious,
face tanned, new runners on a shelf beneath the trolley.

We light a candle and the sound
of your breathing is a motor running down.

Your hand in mine, I study how familiar lines
on your palm – heart, head, life, fate –
curve, cross and veer off in another direction.

.

to keep walking is to swim against myself

The House in Old Bawn

Late on Christmas day, you bring your children to their father's place
turning away from the closed door; it strikes you how dark

night is. How hard to see your way back to the rented house
with its unhinged gate and an overgrown holly bush in the garden.

Inside, shiny purple wallpaper. A puffed-out headrest on the couch
makes you bend your head, hunch up confessor-like.

On the radio, Mary Coughlan sings 'I Can't Make You Love Me'.
You prepare food, eat, watch a film with Brad Pitt.

He looks like Mick when you met him, both of you so young
outside Mulligan's in the snow; kisses beneath a red umbrella.

You scrape away layers of old wallpaper, hang new lemon strips,
smooth out puckers with an un-ringed hand.

A therapist in your head advises 'Now is the time to care
for yourself.' Cold ashes in the grate. Wind moaning through
    the holly bush.

Going to the Well

Three wells,
as in a fairytale;
the first well is dry,
the second well is dry,
the third well is dry.

A woman asks if there is a well committee,
someone to tell where the water went.

We are thirsty then, desperate for a drink.

A woman climbs down into the well
begins to dig with an old tin cup.

We wait for a trickle,
some hint of moisture to wet our lips
with whatever cure there is.

She holds it up,
we lean forward to see
but in the cup there is only money.

Until the Young are Reared

I

Jackdaws in the chimney, their young
tchack tcacking and squeaking,
parents flying in from the fields, insects
and apple blossoms dropping from their beaks.

I walk in and out with the laundry.
Swallows skim the crown of my head,
their clay hive in the corner of the outhouse
above the washing machine.

The birds have taken over the house.

Pigeons ate through the wire
we'd placed across the pigeonhole.
They're in the attic now, gloating,
cooing and coughing.

The other night the chimney caught fire.
You poured water in behind the wooden lintel.
'They've made a bloody bonfire in there.
God knows what they're up to.'

Paddy Mac came to investigate,
'You can put a cap on one side of the chimney
but maybe we should wait until the young are reared
then we'll seal up the pigeonhole as well.

I mean you wouldn't like it if people came
and sealed up your house, and wouldn't let you back in?
'No,' we agreed, thinking about the split mortgage
'we wouldn't like that. We wouldn't like that at all.'

II

Once upon a time my stilt-walking
circus friend lived in the back of a truck,
rearing her young there in the woods,
until the farmer's wife told on them.

They rented a house but the owner
warned that they had to leave,
my friend was eight and a half months pregnant
and Christmas on the way.

The seven-year-old had a sort of pagan
first holy communion. She wanted a white dress
like all her friends. Celebrating her,
they hung ribbons from the blackthorn.

The owners didn't like that, didn't like that at all.

'It's impossible,' I said,
'what with the rents and the gombeens.'
'Yes,' Claire said, 'they won't let us settle
but they won't let us travel either.'

Postcards from Lesvos

'You have to understand,
That no-one puts their children in a boat
Unless the water is safer than the land'
—Warsan Shire

Rima, the Syrian baby, is sleeping
in a vegetable crate hanging from an olive tree.
Just the day before, a Turkish coast guard speeding around them,
swamping their dinghy with waves of seawater,
voices rising, beseeching, 'Allah Akbar, Allah Akbar.'
Children crying, a mother screaming;
'You are going to kill us. You are going to kill us.'

In Exodus the waiter brings us bottles of Mythos.
He has a tattoo on his neck: an eye crying blood.
'It is an old Japanese thing,' he says,
'you can only use this symbol if you've seen someone die.'
On the beach the children who survive are clapping, singing
'We will, we will rock you.' Still wearing life jackets –
Spiderman for the boys, pink Barbie ones for the girls.

Return from Lesvos

To walk into Mahon Falls
is to face the empty page
with a mind full of jabber.

Wind takes my ears
and the waterfall is just a sliver,
fifty sheep away.

The Autumn equinox is behind me
and a shadow moves, bird-shaped,
on the shorn land.

I have come a long way,
from a white and indigo island,
past the holy wells, Kilrossanty Hall
and along the magic road.

Someone cut down the prayer tree
and a new sapling is weighed down
with shoes, ribbons, rosaries, a black bra.

To keep walking is to swim against myself.

I climb upwards,
lie in close to the rocks,
the spray light on my burnt skin.

If my pelvis were to shatter now
you could read the runes
in the pattern of my bones.

When I Visit Dalal

She feeds me homemade biscuits, chocolate, dates and Syrian
    coffee,
shows me the fig tree she planted in the garden.

I pick dandelions, tell her the leaves are good to eat.
Her bare feet are high-arched and strong.

She reads me her story and I type it up on the laptop.
We stop and she hands me a tissue;

a description of her husband Amer crossing the freezing river,
going under, holding the child up out of the water.

Sometimes we get angry; the farmer in Iraq
who sold them slices of mouldy bread

charged a hundred to each family
sheltering from snow and rain in his sheep shed.

'There's greedy people in all countries,' I say.
She nods – 'unkind people, yes, but also kind.'

Dalal looks up words she doesn't know on Google Translate;
gas cooker, lifejacket, ferry, Embassy. We search for films

and photographs; the camp in Iraq,
the state of the tents, row after row unending.

Her daughter Nazha writes her story. She loves pink,
every shade and the colour suits her long dark hair.

Aziz and Judi curl up on the couch to look at a book.
I think about cold, fire, water, blankets, medicine,

long lines for toilets, showers, clothes, food.
Dalal carried heavy buckets of water, armfuls of wood.

Now she reads her story – translating it into English
as I type. Amer works in the local bakery and outside

the people in Cappoquin go about their Saturday,
this woman amongst them.

Shaping the Clay

I find Mary in Whiting Bay with a red bucket
and a shovel for clay washed up by the storm.

In her studio on the cliff above Ardmore,
near the wild garlic path to the well,

she uses a dishwashing brush to work
the slurry of clay and water through a sieve.

When the gorse is Easter gold
and the chocolate-coloured clay is ready,

she cuts a piece with catgut and weighs it
on an old-fashioned scales from Quaine's shop.

She stands at the table, feet warm
in lime-green socks and purple Birkenstocks,

a paint-splashed apron to protect her clothes,
a turquoise bandana around her head.

Her hands, tanned and stained, kneading,
folding, shaping the clay into a cube,

pliable and ready for throwing.
The dance begins;

right foot pushing down on the pedal,
hands centring the lump, finding the base, the depth,

the tips of her fingers pulling up the walls,
head nodding in time to the wheel,

she uses callipers to measure the width; nine inches,
a wet piece of chamois to round off the rim,

an old credit card to straighten the edge,
a bamboo tool from Malawi to level the base.

'Clay fired in a kiln,' she says, 'transforms into pottery.'

When the Buddha bowl is ready she takes a fine paintbrush dipped
in blue, then turquoise. Tip-tipping the brush along the outside
    and inside,

seven hundred and ninety-six times, one dot for every baby
searched for when they dug through the cesspit in Tuam.

Mary hands me the bowl and I take it home.
In the morning I light a candle, place it in the centre.

Flame flickers through clay, each dot a pinprick of sky.

This Haunting   A Spell

The dried herbs she used for healing we sewed into tiny pillows
　　of prayer,
tied them to the hawthorn as carefully as she took her own life,
　　　　　　　　　　　　though she regretted this,
　　　　　　　　　　she told us later in our dreams.

　　Alone the darkness got her in this country where her mother
　　　　　　　　　　was jailed in a convent laundry.
Anna taken from her, too small to say no but small enough to cry

　　　　　　　　and four times more likely to take
　　　　　　　　her own life; this haunting, a spell.

　　You people who came for her remedies and whispered your
　　　　　　　　　　grubby secrets – Anna knew you
the way her mother knew whose semen and blood stains were
　　　　　　　　　　　　　on the town's sheets.

　　　Then, same as always, you turned – a mindless mob
　　　　　　　　　　condemning the likes
of her – the herbalists, the healers with lifetimes in their eyes,

　　　　　　the ones you fear and spit upon again,

push to the margins, push to the edge.

When Saskia Danced

She began by swirling her long dark hair. Shoulders followed,
    then hips, legs, feet
until she was spinning, arms outstretched, around tent, room, field.

I saw her dance with a yellow scarf beside the gorse near
    Coumshingaun Corrie Lake,
like Cathy back with her lover under the waterfall in Mahon
    Falls, in a circle of women

on a cliff above the Aegean.

She danced in a silk skirt from India embroidered with gold,
    red, blue
and silver threads, rippling and spinning Greek light. Revolving
    around her heart

in a trance of bone, muscle, flesh.

A mandala of coloured sand carefully blown onto the surface
    by monks
in orange robes, days and days

of spirals, circles.

Each time her feet touched ground she stamped one grain of sand,
all the months of her life as she raised her son and loved
    the men she loved.

When Saskia danced, others stopped to watch.

A rainy day we gathered in an open-sided tent in East Clare
   to dance for her
though none of us could dervish twirl

to music she loved;

African drums, bodhrans, violins, cymbals, dumbek, pipes, kirtans,
Ave Maria as rain fell on the roof and on the oak Michael said

was strong enough to hold our grief.

Sirens

'You hear? It throbbed, pure, purer, softly and softlier'
—James Joyce, *Ulysses*

The children are singing
a high-pitched song about fish in the trees.

A wing across her left shoulder-
Min's white-blonde hair. Shona's hair, seaweed wild with curls,

A day in Sean Phobal,
Mansfield's daffodil field above the sea.

Our dance, a homage to the women
they called unmarried mothers.
We danced, pegged sheets on a line between apple trees.

Bumps just visible,
Clara was pregnant with Min, Laura with Shona, baskets on
hips they moved

through the other women.
A great day for drying. Sheets cauled above us sang softly for
unheard lullabies,

softlier for babies lost;
Anna whispered, 'I was one of those babies.'

'Fish in the trees, flying fish in the trees,'
Min and Shona sing, climb up through apples to a tree house.

Mermaids swim through mothers.
Below us the Blackwater Valley, river entering this sea, these children.

The Salmon are Standing

The young warrior Fionn didn't mean to steal knowledge. He
    just burst the blister
on the scale of a mythical salmon roasting over the fire, sucked
    his thumb
and knowledge entered him.

More Warriors: Setanta, Brian Boru, Sarsfield, Red Hugh,
    Hugh Dubh, Wolfe Tone,
Robert Emmet, Daniel O'Connell, Parnell, Father Murphy,
    Padraig Pearse; Michael Collins, de Valera.

Cowboys shooting at ceilings yelling 'Yee Haw', standing in
    dusty streets, arms akimbo,
right hand near the holster, ready to draw. I wanted, did not
    want, to be a saloon girl
in a flounced red petticoat,

followed by a bandy-legged cowboy up the wooden stairs to
    bed. Better to be flagellated
in *Mutiny on the Bounty,* better to be a warrior than a fish.
Because The Salmon of Knowledge, *An Bradán Feasa* was Sabdh,

and the sacred pool where she swam. And the Hazel tree
    shedding nuts and leaves into the pool. She could be a
    salmon, a deer, Bridget, Gobnait or Leah and Bovemal who
    shared their plant wisdom with Fionn. In all my years in school,

I never once heard the word goddess, Greek or Irish, until I
    found the versions collected door to door by Ella Young.
Before salmon leave salt water for sweet, they pause. The Salmon
are standing, the fishermen say.

When the warriors dived naked into the pool we could not
   follow. We had to go there at night, bring herbs and
   wildflowers: St John's Wort for depression, sage for heavy
   bleeding, hot flushes, raspberry leaf for labour,

rock rose for terror, buttercup for loss, walnut for change,
   centaury for a strong will, larch
to find a voice, self-heal ... we brought the children with us
   chanting Bríd Bríd Breathe. We stood and we stood – then
   we leapt.

body to body, breath in breath

Sounds

In the mornings Miriam takes her son Peter out in a small
  yellow dinghy.
He lies across it on his tummy, legs stick out like a swallow's tail
then dip into the water as she pushes him across the bay.

Craft sail from the beach below the church in Abbeyside
to the Cunnigar. The sea this morning is corrugated iron,
no break in the clouds. Miriam wades through seaweed.

In time, he will learn to row despite what the neurologists say.
The rhythm of the waves is within, his people were fishermen.
His fear of loud noise, his roars, quieted here.

She walks, pushes, he leans his cheek on the side of the dinghy,
the sea passing through and beneath them, all the way to Helvic.

Karen's boy Derek would never sleep as a baby, unless
she had the Hoover running or a hairdryer. She burnt out
three hairdryers and two Hoovers putting him to sleep.

Such a big baby, the dome of his head covered in a fuzz of blonde,
round blue eyes. She was only nineteen pushing the pram away
then back towards her, away and back, then rocking rocking

in the sitting room with the swirly patterns; a rented house in
  Tallaght.
The noise reminded me of Mam in a temper cleaning. Over the hum
we chatted, drank instant coffee, a cream slice for me, a
  doughnut for her.

Now Derek is a young man trying to breathe in intensive care.
  The sound
of the ventilator will soothe him, the deep sea, the sound of the womb.

47

In the Time of No Touch

after Quarantine by Eavan Boland

When hospital staff couldn't hold the hands
of the dying, and their families
were forbidden to see and touch them,

nurses filled plastic gloves with warm water,
placed one over and one under the dying person's hand,
to mimic the pressure, the warmth

of a living hand. The Hand of God they called it.

You had to stay overnight in the hospital in Waterford.
The porter wheeling you through corridors said
'At night everyone can move freely

but during the day a hundred security guards.'

And the masked guards stopped us on the way
to and from the hospital. Where have you been?
Where are you going? Who did you touch?

I couldn't see their faces but their hands were bare.

I saw the photograph; the age-spotted hand
like grandad's, my father's,
held by balloons shaped like hands.

In the time of no touch
I held the ones I love
body to body, breath in breath, breast to breast.

Devotion

Birds on a prayer tree
descend to the feeder
you have filled

the same way
you put daffodils
in our rooms.

Comfort
when we gather
each morning.

Moments in meditation
before we open our eyes,
speak,

offer dreams
like gold
from silted rivers.

Then we part
each
to a separate

room
pen
story

until the evening
when we return
like strands

of a plait,
across, under, over,
fair, dark-brown, chestnut.

In your house below
Sliabh na mBan:
we three.

Until She Was Only

Antoinette used to ring me from Lahinch,
lonely but singing songs she'd learnt in South America,
teaching yoga, making Brigid's crosses.

The morning she was buried someone blew into a conch,
and there was a horse, white and strange and waiting
on the cliff. Lashing that day, beating and soaking
my back until the rainbow dancers came around and gave
    me shelter.

Someone sang, it's not often you hear
Brazilian songs in the rain.
When the conch opened the air
I knew she was gone.

She used to make sand sculptures like poems.
A pregnant woman … over and over she shaped her,
photographed the tide coming in, the evening light,
especially the light and the way waves began to take

her hair, her features, then her limbs,
until there was only her swollen belly,
the water coursing in around and then over,
until she was only a smooth bump of sand.

My Mother's Lover

After Dad died, the occupational therapist
who came to visit left an invalid toilet seat with handles
in the bathroom and a gadget with a claw hand
to pick up things from the floor.

My mother demonstrated how they worked,
rehearsing to be an old lady
hobbling on arthritic feet.

Until Stein arrived,
the sailor she'd had an affair with
thirty years before.

'You have no idea how angry your father was.'
'I do. I was in the next bedroom.'

And so the Dutchman came back, with flowers
and still wearing her Claddagh ring.
He had blue eyes and a dog called Bonny.

The invalid toilet seat vanished.
She made Emer go shopping for new underwear.

My Dream Out

I search for its name
and realise that it is flying
straight for me.

It lands in my arms
mysterious at a distance, and up close;
wing and wind, down and water.

A back that I could climb upon,
to be taken
to the edge of all that I have known.

I wake on that hesitation.

I take a break from your bedside.
Drive by the takeaway in Sandymount,
remember my last words to you:
'Get well and we'll go for chips.'

I stop now.

Two swans fly in low.

'There's my dream out,' you used to say;
or 'Get up quick, I dreamt last night
the Mohalleys travelled up from Cork.
We need to clean the house.'

Sure enough, they'd arrive that evening,
house clean, food in the cupboard;
as if we always lived like that.

Legacy

Grafton Street, your town: flower-sellers, blue tulips
that can't be real, though you preferred a bought show of these

to the wildflowers from my garden and the ballet-dress roses
I robbed in Avoca, brought fresh and scented to the Home.

Coffee and a coffee slice in Bewley's, my purse full because
you danced like Cher's mama for the money they'd throw.

All the times you bailed me out; Sunday lunches in the Mill House,
clothes, rent, two weddings, cheques in the post.

A busker is singing; *I've seen fire and I've seen rain ...
but I always thought...*

At the Luas, a girl stops begging, shows me where to put money
in the new machine. I press the screen for a ticket: *Adult,*

Stillorgan, where my car is parked, and I'll drive past
your house, the For Sale sign, before heading south.

Bones

'Burn up the corsets. … Make a bonfire of the cruel steels …'
—Elizabeth Stuart Phelps Ward (1873)

Mam used to wear a girdle – a roll-on – a corset. I watched her roll it up over hips and belly to her waist, as I held onto the bed and pulled myself up to stand. On stage she kicked her legs high, wearing a boned satin leotard. Corset is a diminutive of the old French *cors,* meaning 'body', from the Latin *corpus;* corset then means 'little body'. Romantic novels described how the hero encircled the heroine's waist with his hands. At age sixteen, I measured mine – twenty-two inches in tight, denim jeans. Corsets used whalebone, reed, ivory and then metal. Mothers often corseted and tight-laced their girl children, even as they slept, so they would have tiny waists despite the damaged or rearranged internal organs. Because of a torn meniscus I am deepening my studies in somatic movement, trying to become more aware of habitual movements that injure my joints. Soma means 'body', somatic movement is about sensing how the body feels from the inside and not as it is perceived in the mirror or by the audience. I can't bend my knee fully. I wouldn't be able to kneel the way my grandmother did in the church pew, her childbearing hips decently corseted, her head covered. I watch a somatic movement teacher demonstrate how the back is weakened when we pull in our bellies and remember following Mam down the aisle of a restaurant. She had a walker then and her pelvis was twisted, her feet and legs didn't work properly. It was difficult and painful for her to stand and sit. She was raging at her body but the make-up was perfect and she knew how to smile and pose for a photograph. Once I floated in the cradle of her pelvis. I hold the kitchen table to stand, walk slowly across the flagstones. My knee pops, clicks like a shaman's rattle. I blow smoke into the bones of my mother and she turns more easily in the earth.

The Return

for Louise

These are the ways you come back;
the piano returned to you, songs you compose,
a monologue about suffering you learn by heart.
Mother and toddler group, Zumba, a daily walk.

Nights, all of you, sleeping in close together.
Her wild hair that you wash and tend, Bunny,
Sylvanian Families, Winnie the Pooh, Peter Rabbit.

Plants on the kitchen window,
new candles, an oilcloth. Cushions
the colour of burnt orange, amber light, a red throw.

Meals you plan and prepare,
weeding around the snowdrops,
walls lime-washed, clothes on the line.

Each day you set out in your Nissan Micra,
a small car for such courage, a light crowning the hill.

Cherry Blossoms

I walk barefoot to the hen house,
lift the door, reach
into a sanctuary of straw,
find the egg warm
in the cup of my hand.

The new hen still cuckling,
I drop the egg into a pot of water,
butter toast, measure time.

Everything stops as I eat,
my stale thoughts and musty breath

and I remember
Ellie Byrne and me
looking up through cherry blossoms
at stars and the young night,

our warm round bellies
before the eggs
began to fall.

drips of light, small claps of colour

The Cherry Blossoms Were Purple There

That Autumn, Australian spring,
in the forest where we camped
the trees were full of coloured birds
with strange cries and calls
and mosquitoes that bit the legs off you.

In the ocean, waves came in sideways
across our hips and there was a rip
that could drag you out to sea,
indigo jellyfish with ferocious stings.

We ate mangoes for breakfast,
raisin toast and coffee in the café;
tame parrots, white and green and pink
croaked helloo helloo.

Every evening we walked through the woods.
There, we said, looking up at the dozy koalas.
Tea-tree and Eucalyptus drip-dripped
their juices into the lake, bark peeled
and shed itself. We hung our clothes from the branches.

In Dante's House

*'The Lord willed the woman, Beatrice, to eat Dante's heart
which she did hesitantly.'*
—Dante's *La Vita Nuova and the Vision of the Eaten Heart*

There's a painting of you and Beatrice
meeting that second time,
hands outstretched, faces like daisies.

How can breathing flesh compete?
She's always twenty-four years old;
a phantom woman waiting

for mid-life
this winter day,
her opening throat; your heart.

Upstairs, projected images:
you and her in Hell;
Purgatory; Heaven.

Wings
around the void
which becomes a host,

a spinning light in the heart of Florence.
Shops: designer shoes, bags,
clothes, perfume, jewels.

A bicycle bell trings in the street below;
a young woman runs up the stone stairs.
And I give up. All the ways I tried to be loved.

A Copper Basin in Florence

The owner smiles as if she knows me
and pulls out a chair. Beside the doorway
a copper basin lies on its side. Nana Ross had one
just like it, in the kitchen, behind the grocery shop.

As a child I imagined my soul was that colour
and sanctifying grace was red, dripping
rosary-like, a kind of divine sweat or smelled
of frankincense, myrrh, milk and straw.

By age nine I had committed a mortal sin,
let Nicki Walshe touch me there and didn't tell,
made a bad confession, took Communion
paper thin and white on my black-spotted tongue.

Nana sprinkled us with holy water,
gave me a blessed rosary from Lourdes,
all blue and purple it was, but I lost it
like I lost the library book, sins mounting up;

the row over contraception with a priest
in the confessional box in Stillorgan.
Sister Anne, white musty face, those thin lips
'How dare you, a girl, question holy men.'

Lying bare-breasted in the long grass with Ciarán,
drinking Guinness followed by Harvey Wallbangers,
vomiting it all up on Pearse Street,
a guy from Tuam holding my forehead.

Walking away from my father's house, my marriage,
my job, to dance barefoot in a circle of women
who prayed with wrists, hips, feet and drums,
bellies painted gold, Magdalene red.

In the Duomo di Firenze the air stinks of old blood,
paintings heavy with pigment and suffering,
I rinse my mouth with the Signora's wine
and that copper basin is only a basin, a thing.

Leaving Florence

On the plane – through the window
the sun begins to set above clouds.

'Look,' I say. You glance and smile,
go back to your book.

The sunset turns
a deep and heartbreaking amber.

The painting of two ordinary women
in the Uffizi.

One in a skirt made from emeralds,
the other's dress a slice of this sky.

'Look,' I say, desperate

for the casual
years granted.

Be with me now

as amber fades to palest peach
and the plane begins to curve away from the sun.

Careful

Rough dreams clenched in my jaw, still in bed
when the cat pounces, blood on breath from the night hunt,

a paw on my cheek. Oh how I love her soft paw on my cheek.
It took so long to befriend her, to touch fur, be touched,

but her breath, the scent of blood, her claws ...

I hear you in the other room, laughing on Zoom, at work,
while we purr into each other.

Later I peel skin, cut, chop beetroot for soup,
see how red my fingers when I touch your face.

Touched

Last night it woke me, a thimble of light cutting
through the slit in the curtain, on your side of the bed.

You slept on, unaware of its still nesting
like the white sea glass we found on Curragh strand.

It must have affected you all the same;

two hares rose up in the field beyond,
a vixen cried out, her throat full of moon.

And I touched the silver thumbprint on the back of your head.

Medicine for December

More bad news on the radio.
Another endangered tree,
sucked dry, burnt, chopped down.

Antoinette brought me a present from Ethiopia,
an incense burner, a crooked pot, indentations –
fingers in the red clay baked hard by the sun.

She said that the Ethiopian people take only what they need,
cut the bark, gather resin, make ritual, give thanks,
burn incense and serve coffee with salty popcorn.

In the chapels of childhood I cuddled into Gran,
nuggets in a crucible. Smoke censing the air.
A thurible swinging forward and back.

After birth, gold, frankincense, myrrh,
mysterious shapes in my mouth,
a journey measured out in stars.

The Book of Exodus prescribes
frankincense to be ground and burnt before the Ark
of the Covenant in the wilderness Tabernacle.

This oil embalmed bodies in Egyptian tombs,
dates all the way back to Babylon,
a solace for grief, a pulmonary antiseptic.

Sycamores and pines sway forward and back,
thorn trees claw at the sky. Far from this place
Boswellia sacra – barkstripped, oozing, milksap hardening.

Inhaling, my lungs find the cut where they used to be,
Gran drinking water from the holy well, prayer rags on the blackthorn
and Mam's mythical cornflower – a blue we'd never see.

Exhaling, they leave again.
Inhaling, I breathe with leaves and trees
that bleed more slowly and more sweetly than we ever will.

At Dusk, At Dawn

'… at dawn and dusk. I lie in the dark
wondering if this quiet in me now
is a beginning or an end.'
— Jack Gilbert

You fall asleep in the armchair
a red scarf around your sore throat
this evening in January; halfway
between your birthday and mine,

your breath, the spaces between.
And that we would land up here,
half-way between Waterford and Cork,
in a Gaeltacht, a hobbit cottage.

In a while I will get up and begin dinner.
Close the curtains and drink wine.
You will prepare for bed earlier than I,
leave the dog out to gallop through the night field.

I will switch off lights. Read and doze in my bath.
Climbing in beside you I'll be cold
then too hot; when you made the bed
you shook the duvet feathers over to my side.

In the morning I will wake and hear you in the kitchen,
radio on. That old Fleetwood Mac song – *building*
my life around you ... The cat heavy against my hip,
our books piled up either side of the bed.

ecstasy zinging through flesh, our blood

Landscape of the Body

I haven't climbed through this tunnel of pink sienna
and moss-green rocks to the secret beach in Ballymacart

for a long time now, to explore the cave where Susie danced
that day emerging from the darkness, drawing a chain

with her feet in the sand, a chord linking back to wombed cave.
So still she was in that moment.

Aisling on the cliff, a stream falling behind her, hennaed hair,
roots at the parting, lime striated through red-pink stone.

Claire and Louise, balancing like herons in the sea.
I saw a bird in the rock, traced her wings. You can't fly

through stone, I thought, but what did I know,
down on all fours digging in the sand.

You played the djembe and sang about a dragon,
Gwen lay back in the waves, her copper hair dark with sea.

Shane caught mackerel. We roasted them on sticks over the fire,
ate them from our hands, lemon and salt from our fingers.

I Wore It All Summer

A shop on the main street in Newbridge, a cranky man from India,
reams of scarves, wrap-around silk skirts, genie trousers,

a cotton dress, dyed with Tamil Nadu Indigo, a scalloped hem,
tiny shells hand-sewn where indigo meets blue.

Somewhere a seamstress paid a pittance for the task,
sewed each shell along a swirl of tie-dye,

making a sea of that dress. The clink and tinkle
of bangles gold and warm around her arms.

I wore it when I met you in your flat in Harold's Cross.
The fabric smelled musky, pearl buttons down the front

you opened one by one. I wore it all summer. We both remember
the dress, my long hair, how we knew the way to dance together,

shells clicking, scalloped skirt swinging around tanned legs. Soft
cotton growing softer, blue running into rinse water, fading
    over time.

Flesh

The women go swimming at dawn
in Glencairn, Clonea, Ballyquin, Goat Island;
Mary, Brenda, Judy, Charlotte, Elaine.
Sea wind on flushed sleepy skin, cold slap of the waves.

Afterwards the women drink Ethiopian coffee,
warm and spicy. Spray each other
with geranium, rose and juniper oil.
Lemon air peels over bodies

that have given birth, made milk,
bled over and over, charged and depleted,
the constant pull and push
in a world that never suited them anyway.

Now this giving in to flesh and bone,
tide and wind. Every morning
the women gather on the wet sand
and they run whooping into the waves.

Wildsong

You and I were walking through the old Church.

'I used to sing in the choir here,' I said, that same
feeling – music and voice as prayer – between us.

There was somewhere we needed to be
and I remembered which door was the quickest way.

My fifteen-year-old self was singing with the others.
I nodded over at her – throat pulsing like a bird's.

Then you and I went out amongst the people,
so many of them at the festival, or was it a fair?

Delicious food – manna and garments
of every colour, embroidered with silver.

I chose white, you handed me a swan feather
and a tiny indigo cup of medicine.

I sipped songs from dolphins and seals,
bent down and picked a buttercup, held it

under your chin, a gleam of gold on your throat.

Below the Cliffs in Doolin

A woman said 'If you swim into that cave,
eels will wind around your body and squeeze the life out of ye.'

In wetsuits, cool guys slapped the skin of the sea,
signalling to the dolphin.

Families standing on the cliffs and rocks above leaned forward.

Suddenly, a dolphin shadow below,
the slip of her skin against mine.

The sea changed, I swear to you the substance
of water and blood changed and chuckled around our bones,

we smiled at each other, laughed like children
jumping waves, all cool dudeness, all shyness gone.

The dolphin stole a ball and tossed it in the air,
someone caught it, threw it back.

Balancing the ball on her snout
she flew out to sea away from the sheltering rocks.

People on the cliffs ran to the edge to see what would happen next.

Back she came and scooped a young woman
up on her back, swimming out to sea again.

A helicopter came roaring above; through a megaphone
a man shouted down at us: 'STEP BACK FROM THE EDGE.

GET OUT OF THE WATER. THAT DOLPHIN IS WILD.
DO NOT TOUCH THE DOLPHIN.'

We weren't safe, they said, the cave with the eels behind us,
the open sea ahead, and the dolphin wild as anything,

a woman on her back, the dolphin's eye, the laughs of her
ecstasy zinging through flesh, our blood.

Someone could have fallen, true,
that day when I realised what transubstantiation means.

Pulse, Beat, Breath

'It is rhythm that makes the birds fly, it is rhythm that makes the creatures of the earth walk.'
—Hazrat Inayat Khan, *The Law of Rhythm*

This is what the mystics mean when they speak of being
present. Now – toe heel, toe heel stomp – slide.

Michelle onstage with other young men and women,
combining tap dance rhythms with African drums.

Playing, building, layer upon layer – shuffle hop step
shuffle hop step, stomp-pickup-step-step-brush-hopstep.

Arms akimbo, my daughter laughs – 'If you think you lose it,'
she says, 'some other part of you has to do it' – that split second

when her shoe strikes a fraction of a beat behind another's.
Toe-taps ricochet off wood, hands bounce on goatskin.

A thunder of feet; bombershays cramp rolls drawbacks flaps
scuffs-shuffle-slides-spank-slap-stomp HEY!

Silence. Dust rising in the spotlight. Bodies pulling in breath.

ACKNOWLEDGEMENTS

The author wishes to thank the publishers and editors of the following magazines, journals and radio programmes where a number of these poems, or versions of them, previously appeared: *Southword, The Stinging Fly, Poetry Ireland Review, Poetry, The Irish Times, Portland Review, Poetry Wales, Orbis, Solas, Channel, Amphibian Lit, Abridged, Mslexia, Vanguard's 14, Poethead, The Waxed Lemon, Poets Meet Politics, A New Ulster, Waterford Healing Arts, The Craft Council of Ireland, Reflection – The Irish Hospice Foundation, Poetry Out Loud, Words Lightly Spoken, Ó Bhéal Poetry Film* and *Moving Poems* Special thanks to RTÉ's *Sunday Miscellany* programme.

'When I Visit Dalal' won the Poetry Ireland Trócaire Prize in 2022.

Poems also appeared in the following anthologies: *Children of the Nation, Halleluiah for 50ft Women,* edited by Raving Beauties (Bloodaxe Books, 2015); *Children of the Nation,* edited by Jenny Farrell (Culture Matters, 2019); *Ten Poems for Breakfast,* selected and introduced by Ana Samson (Candlestick Press, 2019); *Staying Human,* edited by Neil Astley (Bloodaxe Books, 2020); *Poems from Pandemia,* edited by Patrick Cotter, (The Munster Literature Centre, 2020); *Emergence,* edited by Shane O'Hanlon and Paul Finucane (Redbarn Publishing, 2020); *Local Wonders,* edited by Pat Boran (Dedalus Press, 2021); *Romance Options,* edited by Leanne Quinn and Joseph Woods (Dedalus Press, 2022); *Washing Windows Too,* edited by Alan Hayes (Arlen House, 2022); *Washing Windows III,* edited by Alan Hayes (Arlen House, 2023).

The author is grateful to the Arts Council of Ireland, the Arts Office, Waterford City and County, and ArtLinks, to Poetry Ireland Introductions and the team at Poetry Ireland, in particular Elizabeth Mohen, the staff of the Tyrone Guthrie Centre, the Molly Keane Writers Retreats, Waterford Libraries and librarians, my colleagues in Waterford Healing Arts and *Réalta,* the National Body for Arts and Health, Creative Ireland and Creative Waterford.

For their skill, wisdom and generosity, thanks and appreciation to editor Pat Boran, and to mentors and friends: Arts Officer Margaret Organ, Grace Wells, Mark Roper, Thomas McCarthy, Don Share and producer Sarah Binchy.

For creative collaboration and warm friendship, love and gratitude to: Virginia Keane, Mary Lys Carbery, Sinéad Hannon, Marlene French Mullen, Fiona Aryan, Paul Casey, Mary Grehan, Fergal O' Connor, Susie Lamb, Joanne Boyle, Gwen McHale, Richard Skinner, Will Nugent, Mary Lincoln and the community of writers, editors and artists in the South East and beyond.

Love and gratitude to my beloved John and my family – for so much.